Funniest Bone Animal Jokes

SILLY Cat JOKES to Tickle Your FUNNY BONE

Doreen Gonzales

Enslow Elementary

an imprint of

Enslow Publishers, Inc.
40 Industrial Road
Box 398
Berkeley Heights, NJ 07922
USA

http://www.enslow.com

Enslow Elementary, an imprint of Enslow Publishers, Inc.

Enslow Elementary® is a registered trademark of Enslow Publishers, Inc.

Library of Congress Cataloging-in-Publication Data

Gonzales, Doreen.
   Funniest bone animal jokes : silly cat jokes to tickle your funny bone / Doreen Gonzales.
      pages cm. — (Funniest bone animal jokes)
   Includes index.
   Summary: "Read jokes, limericks, tongue twisters, and knock-knock jokes about house cats and other types of cats. Also find out fun facts about these animals"—Provided by publisher.
   ISBN 978-0-7660-5991-7
   1. Cats—Juvenile humor. 2. Wit and humor, Juvenile. I. Title.
   PN6231.C23G66 2014
   818'.5402—dc23
                              2013015587

Future editions:
Paperback ISBN: 978-0-7660-5992-4   EPUB ISBN: 978-0-7660-5993-1
Single-User PDF ISBN: 978-0-7660-5994-8   Multi-User PDF ISBN: 978-0-7660-5995-5

Printed in the United States of America
072014 HF Group, North Manchester, IN
10 9 8 7 6 5 4 3 2 1

To Our Readers: We have done our best to make sure all Internet addresses in this book were active and appropriate when we went to press. However, the author and the publisher have no control over and assume no liability for the material available on those Internet sites or on other Web sites they may link to. Any comments or suggestions can be sent by e-mail to comments@enslow.com or to the address on the back cover.

Every effort has been made to locate all copyright holders of material used in this book. If any errors or omissions have occurred, corrections will be made in future editions of this book.

Illustration Credits: Clipart.com, pp. 4 (top), 5 (top), 7 (top), 8 (middle), 14 (top), 15 (top), 23 (top), 28 (top), 30 (top), 34 (top, middle left), 35 (top), 36 (top), 37 (middle right, bottom), 38 (top); Shutterstock.com: p. 39 (bottom); abracadabra, pp. 9 (middle), 17 (bottom); Amplion, p. 19 (middle); Anton Brand, p. 32 (top); artist-ka, p. 11 (top); Bananaboy, p. 41 (top); baza178, p. 7 (bottom); The Blue Planet, p. 40 (top); cartoons, p. 25 (bottom); Celana, p. 41 (middle); Chad Champneys, p. 32 (middle); Christos Georghiou, pp. 1, 45; Cindy Hughes, p. 10 (top); Cory Thoman, p. 20 (bottom); Crisan Rosu (all), p. 3; dalmingo, p. 42 (bottom); dedMazay, p. 37 (middle left), 43 (middle); Dennis Cox, p. 7 (middle); elenafoxly, p. 24 (bottom); EMJAY SMITH, p. 9 (top); Forewer, p. 6 (top); HerArtSheLoves, p. 11 (bottom); John T. Takai, p. 5 (bottom); Klara Viskova, pp. 30 (top), 32 (bottom), 33 (bottom); kludmila, p. 20 (top); Konstantin Remizov, p. 13 (bottom); laura.st, p. 12 (bottom); Liusa, p. 12 (top); Lorelyn Medina, pp. 19 (bottom), 40 (bottom right); Lossik, p. 14 (bottom); Maciej Sojka, p. 19 (top); Mahmuttibet, p. 43 (bottom); Matthew Cole, pp. 15 (bottom), 16 (bottom), 23 (middle), 24 (top), 26 (bottom); Memo Angeles, p. 39 (top); MisterElements, pp. 8 (top), 18 (bottom); Morphart Creation, p. 29 (bottom); natsa, p. 43 (top); notkoo, p. 34 (dentist); okili77, p. 13 (middle right); olly, p. 28 (bottom); onime, p. 31 (bottom); pinkkoala, p. 6 (bottom); Pushkin, pp. 8 (bottom), 13 (top), 18 (top), 23 (bottom), 29 (top), 35 (bottom), 40 (bottom left); RAStudio, p. 17 (top); Regissercom, p. 26 (top); Rocket400 Studio, p. 10 (bottom right); sababa66, p. 16 (top); sbego, p. 41 (bottom); sewluang, p. 27 (bottom); Solaie, p. 42 (top); Teguh Mujiono, p. 22 (bottom); Tony Oshlick, p. 11 (middle); VectorShots, p. 36 (bottom); vikici, p. 22 (middle); waihoo, p. 27 (top); Wimpos, p. 5 (middle); Yayayoyo, pp. 14 (middle), 25 (middle), 33 (middle), YRoma, p. 21 (top); © Thinkstock: © Alexey Bannykh/iStock, p. 34 (black panther); © ayelet keshet/iStock, p. 9 (bottom); Frazer Worth/iStock/© Smokeyjo, p. 13 (middle left); © jerry23774/iStock, p. 37 (top); © joannagoldman/iStock, p. 21 (bottom); © jojo100/iStock, p. 10 (bottom left); Purestock, p. 4 © SilkenOne/iStock, p. 27 (middle); © suryadiranau/iStock, p. 31 (top).

Cover Illustrations: © Lo Sik Cheung Stony/iStock/© Thinkstock (front); Chad Champneys/Shutterstock.com (back).

Contents

Ten cats were on a boat and one jumped off. How many were left?

None, they were all copycats!

What kind of cat has eight legs?

Funny felines find fun fooling furry family friends.

An octo-puss.

What noise does a cat make going down the highway?

What do you get when you cross a cat with a canary?

Miaoooooooooooooooooooooow!

Shredded tweet.

How do you stop a ten-pound parrot from talking too much?

Buy a thirty-pound cat.

Knock, knock.

Who's there?

Meow.

Meow who?

Take meow to the ballgame.

Why did the cat family move next door to the mouse family?

So they could have the neighbors for dinner.

Cats chew cheddar cheese and chomp on crunchy fleas.

Cats cannot see in the dark. However, they do see well in dim light. The backs of their eyes are like tiny mirrors that reflect the light and make it brighter. Also, their pupils can expand to be quite large. This lets in lots of light. During the day, these pupils narrow to slits so that they don't let in too much light.

Knock, knock.

Who's there?

Cat.

Cat who?

Cat you open the door? It's cold out here.

Copper cats play patty-cake while cream-colored cats play catch.

What do you call a cat that can bowl?

An alley cat.

2 Kittens

What happens when a kitten goes swimming?

It gets wet.

What do baby cats wear?

Dia-purrrs.

Knock, knock.

Who's there?

Kitten.

Kitten who?

Are you kitten me?

FUN FACT

Kittens are born with their eyes closed. They use their sense of touch and smell to find their mothers. By the second week of life, their eyes have opened. Newborn kittens all have blue eyes. These will change over time into their adult color.

How do mama cats buy clothes for their kittens?

They order them from cat-alogs.

What do kittens like to eat on hot days?

Mice cream cones.

Where is one place that your kitten can sit but you can't?

In your lap.

Kittens' paws pause while their tongues taste treats.

9

Knock, knock.

Who's there?

Three little kittens.

Three little kittens who?

The three little kittens who lost their mittens. Have you seen any?

Who brings kittens presents on Christmas Eve?

Santa Claws.

Who helped Cinderella's kitten go to the ball?

Her furry godmother.

Here's a pretty itty bitty city kitty.

There once was a brave little kitty
Who wanted to visit the city.
She hopped on a bus
But caused such a fuss
That she had to get off—such a pity!

What can a cat have
that a dog can't?

Kittens.

What was the kitten's
favorite color?

Purr-ple.

Cuddly kittens can't
catch clever canaries.

Why did the mother
cat move her kittens?

She didn't
want to litter.

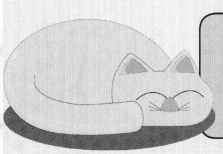

The kitten curled up on the rug
Was fluffy and cute as a bug.
So inviting it seemed,
As it quietly dreamed,
Everyone gave it a hug.

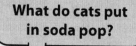

What do cats put in soda pop?

Mice cubes.

Did you put the cat out?

I didn't know it was on fire!

What do you get when you cross a cat with a lemon?

A sour puss!

DID YOU KNOW?

Cats use their whiskers to feel their way around. Whiskers help them move through the dark and figure out if they can fit through an opening. A cat's whiskers also tell others how the cat is feeling. When its whiskers are pointed forward and down, the cat is happy. If they are pulled back on its face, the cat is angry.

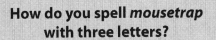
How do you spell *mousetrap* with three letters?

C-A-T.

Where do cats write down notes?

Scratch paper!

Fancy felines find fault with the fearful and forgetful.

Limerick

There once was a big hungry cat
Who spent his time chasing a rat—
Until came the day
The rat moved away,
And that was the end of all that.

What do you call a cat that's been under the hair dryer?

Fluffy.

Knock, knock.

Who's there?

Juan.

Juan who?

Juan day I'll get a cat of my own.

Limerick

The felines all wanted to play.
Their antics included a wide array:
Running and pouncing,
Chasing and bouncing—
They played all night and slept all day.

What do you call an overweight cat?

A flabby tabby.

Knock, knock.

Who's there?

Catsup.

Catsup who?

Catsup a tree and she won't come down.

What did the cat say when he stubbed his toe?

"Meowch."

Choosy cats chew chewing gum while kittens chomp candy chips.

Knock, knock.

Who's there?

Meow.

aid who's there?

Meow.

Speak up. I can't hear you.

Can you hear meow?

Cats at School

How do you know when your cat's been on the Internet?

The mouse has teeth marks in it.

Knock, knock.

Who's there?

Teacher.

Teacher who?

Teacher cat any manners?

What did the cat get on the test?

A purr-fect score.

What's smarter than a cat that can count?

A spelling bee.

DID YOU KNOW?

A cat's tail can communicate how it is feeling. When the tail is standing straight up with its fur flat, the cat is happy. If the fur on its tail is standing out, the cat is angry or frightened. When a cat waves its tail back and forth, it is mad.

How do you spell cat backwards?

C-a-t b-a-c-k-w-a-r-d-s.

Where did the cat class go on a field trip?

To the mew-seum.

What's a cat favorite subject?

Hiss-tory.

There once was a cat named Keller
Who was a fantastic speller.
When he went to school,
The kids called him cool,
And treated him like any old feller.

Knock, knock.

Who's there?

Feline.

Feline who?

Feline going
to school?

"Meow!"

Talented tabbies teach
turtles to talk.

There was a bright feline named Derek
Who could figure out all things numeric.
What is nineteen times sixty?
Then divide it by fifty—
The gift made him a cat mathe-ma-teric.

How does a cat count?

One, mew, three.

Clever cats count cabbages, cashews, and corn chips.

Fantastic felines find physics fabulous.

Why did the mice stay in at recess?

Because it was raining cats and dogs.

5 Lions

What is a lion's favorite kind of beans?

Human beans.

What would you get if you crossed a lion with crushed ice?

A man-eating snowcone.

Little lions like licking lemon lollipops.

What would you get if your crossed a tangerine and a lion?

An orange that nobody picks on.

Why weren't lions given wings?

They asked for chicken nuggets instead.

How does a lion brush his mane?

With a catacomb!

A lion was combing his mane,
But his snarls were causing him pain.
He cut off the fur
That had made him grrr,
And never had tangles again.

How does a lion greet the other animals in his territory?

"Pleased to eat you!"

What should you know if you want to be a lion tamer?

More than the lion.

Lions are the only cats that live in groups. These groups are called prides. A few males, several females, and many young live in a pride. All of the females in a pride are related.

When rampaging lions roar and roam, roving rabbits run for home.

Limerick

His friends thought him kind of a bore
For constantly trying to roar.
But in spite of disfavor,
He kept up the behavior
Until no one was left to ignore.

Knock, knock.

Who's there?

Lionel.

Lionel who?

Lionel eat me if you don't open the door!

6 Tigers

Why do tigers eat raw meat?

Because they can't cook.

Who went into the tiger's lair and came out alive?

The tiger.

DID YOU KNOW?

- The tiger is the world's largest wildcat.
- A tiger's stripes are unique, with no two tigers having the same stripe pattern.
- A tiger's roar can be heard from two miles away.
- Tigers can swim and often lie in streams and pools.

A tiger tiptoed across the tightrope while twirling teacups on his toes.

Knock, knock.

Who's there?

Tiger.

Tiger who?

There's a tiger at your door, and you want to know its name?

On which side does a tiger have the most fur?

The outside.

A tiger named Tina trained typists to type.

Why did the tiger change his socks on the golf course?

He got a hole in one.

Two tigers talked to two talkative toucans.

There was a young lady from Niger
Who smiled as she rode on a tiger.
They returned from the ride
With the lady inside
And a smile on the face of the tiger.

When is the best time to take your pet tiger for a walk?

Any time she wants.

On what day do tigers eat people?

Chewsday.

Knock, knock.

Who's there?

Mia.

Mia who?

Mia tiger—let me in!

What do you get when you cross a canary with a tiger?

I don't know, but you'd better listen when it sings.

A tiger escaped from the zoo
But was confused about what he should do.
He thought he would see
The latest movie,
With candy and soda pop, too.

What's the difference between a tiger and a lion?

A tiger is missing the mane part.

27

Cheetahs and Leopards

Knock, knock.

Who's there?

Miniature.

Miniature who?

Miniature turn your back on a leopard you're in trouble.

How do you make a leopard disappear?

Use spot remover.

DID YOU KNOW?

Leopards have a wide range of coat colors, depending on where they live. Leopards that live in dry areas have tan fur. Those that live in forests have dark fur. The spots on leopards are called rosettes. Some leopards have circular spots, while others have spots that are square. Leopards with black fur are called panthers—although *panther* can also be another name for the mountain lion.

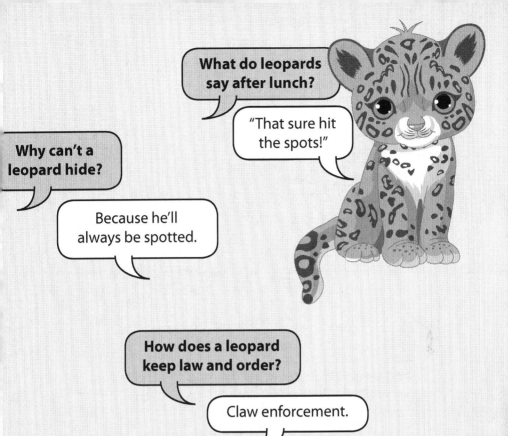

What do leopards say after lunch?

"That sure hit the spots!"

Why can't a leopard hide?

Because he'll always be spotted.

How does a leopard keep law and order?

Claw enforcement.

Limerick

They thought she was making a joke
When she showed up wearing a cloak.
But because of a dream
She thought of this scheme:
She'd hide all her spots with a coat.

Eye doctor: What seems to be the problem?

Leopard trainer: I keep seeing spots before my eyes.

Knock, knock.

Who's there?

Noah.

Noah who?

Noah why there's a cheetah in your yard?

Leaping over lazy leopards leaves little leeway for luck.

Limerick

A leopard named Spotty Louise
Caught a cold and sneezed a huge sneeze.
It left her fur in knots
And blew off all her spots,
And now she's a different species.

Why didn't they let the wildcat into school?

They knew he was a cheetah.

Childish cheetahs chuckle while they cheat at checkers.

Knock, knock.

Who's there?

Cheetah.

Cheetah who?

Cheat-again and I'm quitting.

What do you get when you cross a leopard with a dishwasher?

Spots on your dishes.

Cheetahs and zebras do yoga in togas.

What happened to the cheetah that took a bath everyday?

After a week he was spotless.

Mountain lions are also known as cougars, catamounts, pumas, and sometimes panthers. They like to live alone and are not often seen by people. Mountain lions need a large range of at least 30 square miles (78 square kilometers).

Knock, knock.

Who's there?

A mountain lion.

Wait . . . what?

Mountain lions and marmots are mammals that make homes in the mountains.

What did the scientist say when he discovered a wildcat that was thought to be extinct?

"I've found the missing lynx."

Why does a mountain lion chase its prey?

It loves fast food.

What does a jaguar eat after visiting the dentist?

The dentist.

Jaguars jabber as they jump rope and joke as they jog.

Limerick

There once was an orderly ocelot
Who liked to clean and dust a lot.
His house was dirt-free,
And though he was friendly,
He was seen as a crabby fusspot.

Where was the panther when the sun went down?

In the dark.

Bobcats and wildcats chitchat with tomcats while standing on doormats.

How does a mountain lion say good-bye?

"Catch you later!"

Knock, knock.

Who's there?

Jay.

Jay who?

Jay Gwire. Take me to the zoo.

Limerick

A mountain lion that lived up on high
Grew tired of touching the sky;
So he moved to the beach
Where all he could reach
Were the sand and the sea and his pie.

The Saber-toothed Tiger

What did the saber-toothed tiger say to the mammoth?

"You look a little long in the tooth."

What do you call a saber-toothed tiger who has eaten your mother's sister?

An aunt-eater!

How do you brush the teeth of a saber-toothed tiger?

Very carefully.

A saber-toothed tiger from Tucson had a toothache on Tuesday.

Saber-toothed cats lived from about 56 million years ago to about 12,000 years ago. These prehistoric cats had two long, fanglike teeth up to eight inches long. They used their teeth to catch prey.

What weighs 400 pounds and jumps every five seconds?

A saber-toothed tiger with the hiccups.

Knock, knock.

Who's there?

Emma.

Emma who?

Emma saber-toothed tiger. Can I come in?

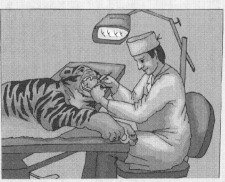

What time is it when a saber-toothed tiger visits the dentist?

Tooth-hurty.

37

Knock, knock.

Who's there?

Shirley.

Shirley who?

Shirley that's not a saber-toothed tiger— they're extinct.

Where did saber-toothed tigers sleep?

Anywhere they wanted.

The saber-toothed tiger's roar rolled around in a rhythmic rumbling.

Limerick

A saber-toothed tiger named Shel
Was determined to learn how to spell.
He enrolled in a school,
But it wasn't too cool
When he forgot to come in at the bell.

The saber-toothed tiger sang softly while sailing safely through icy seas.

What do you call a 400-pound saber-toothed tiger?

Sir.

Limerick

Limerick

The tooth fairy's mind was perplexed,
For the problem was rather complex.
The gigantic tooth
Was too huge to move
So the saber-tooth's tooth was left.

What do saber-toothed tigers call mice?

Delicious.

Limerick

The saber-toothed tigers were told
To move where it wasn't so cold.
But they didn't think
It would make them extinct—
When they stayed, they failed to grow old.

Cats in Hiss-story

On what should you mount a statue of your cat?

On a caterpillar!

The roaring king of the beasts likes to sing while he feasts.

When is it bad luck to see a black cat?

When you're a mouse.

What cat loves rock and roll?

Elvis Purr-esley.

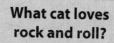

DID YOU KNOW?

Ancient Egyptians considered cats sacred and they worshipped them as gods. During the sixteenth century in Europe, cats were thought to be witches in disguise. In the United States, black cats are thought to bring bad luck. In Japan, Scotland, and England, though, a black cat is thought to bring good luck.

What is the name of the cat that lives near the pyramids?

Cleo-cat-tra.

What do you call it when a witch's cat falls off her broomstick?

A cat-tastrophe.

Knock, Knock.

Who's there?

Hans.

Hans who?

Hans off the witch's cat!

Do black cats bring bad luck or does bad luck bring black cats?

Old MacDonald's cat meowed more than most.

What word did the magician's cat say on stage?

"Abra-cat-dabra!"

Limerick

The cat climbed up on the broom,
Then the witch took off with a zoom.
They flew through the sky
To the moon way up high
And eventually came back, I presume.

Knock, Knock.

Who's there?

Claws!

Claws who?

Santa Claws! I've got your gifts!

Limerick

Cleopatra, the Egyptian queen,
Had regal cats who would constantly preen.
With their fur so sleek
And just enough cheek—
There was no mistaking their self-esteem.

Why did the cat jump over the moon?

She was following the cow.

Make a Limerick Book

Limericks are a fun form of poetry. They were made popular by a writer named Edward Lear. In the 1840s, he wrote *A Book of Nonsense*, which was full of silly limericks. You can create your own book of these short, hilarious poems.

What you will need:

- plain white paper—at least two pieces

- one large loose rubber band or a stapler

- pencil and/or colored markers

Rules for writing a limerick:

- The first, second, and fifth lines rhyme with each other. These lines usually have eight to ten syllables.

- The third and fourth lines rhyme. These lines usually have four to six syllables.

- The first line in a limerick usually ends with a name or place.

- The last line is usually funny or unexpected.

Getting started:

1. Pick a name or place to use in the first line.

2. Use a rhyming dictionary to find words that will go with that first line. These can be used at the end of lines two and five.

3. Write lines one, two, and five first. Then go back and write line three and four. It can be easier that way.

Example:

There was a young lady from Niger
Who smiled as she rode on a tiger.
They returned from the ride
With the lady inside
And a smile on the face of the tiger.

How to create the book:

1. Fold each piece of paper in half crosswise.

2. Place one of the pieces of folded paper in the middle of the other. These will be the pages of your book. You can use more paper. Just continue folding paper and putting the pages together.

3. Slide the rubber band around the paper until it reaches the fold of the paper in the middle of the book. This will hold the pages together. If you prefer, staple the pages along the fold.

4. Write a limerick on each page. Use colored pencils, crayons, or markers to illustrate. Don't forget your title page, with your name as the author!

Words to Know

alley cat—A homeless cat that roams the alleys of a town.

bore—Someone who is not very interesting.

catacomb—An underground cemetery.

catnap—A short nap.

cheek—Nerve or sass.

feline—Having to do with cats or the cat family.

joke—Something that is funny or makes a person laugh.

lair—The den or home of a wild animal.

limerick—A funny poem that is five lines long and follows a special formula.

long in the tooth—Old. The expression comes from the fact that horses' teeth continue to grow as they age.

lynx—A kind of wildcat with long limbs, a short tail, and tufted ears that lives in North America.

mane—The long hair around the head of the male lion.

panther—A large wildcat; another name for a black leopard or a mountain lion.

Persian—A breed of cat that has long hair and a flat face.

sphinx—An ancient statue made of stone in Egypt. The sphinx has a lion's body and a human head.

tongue twister—A sentence or group of words that is hard to say aloud. The sounds sometimes leave one's tongue "twisted."

wildcat—Any of several different kinds of large cats that live in the wild, such as the bobcat, tiger, and ocelot.

Read More

Books

Dahl, Michael. *The Funny Farm: Jokes About Dogs, Cats, Ducks, Snakes, Bears and Other Animals*. Mankato, Minn.: Picture Window Books, 2010.

Elliott, Rob. *Zoolarious Animal Jokes for Kids*. Ada, Mich.: Revell, 2012.

Lederer, Richard, and Jim Ertner. *Super Funny Animal Jokes (Animal Cracker Uppers)*. Portland, Oreg.: Marion Street Press, 2011.

National Geographic Kids. *Just Joking: 300 Hilarious Jokes, Tricky Tongue Twisters, and Ridiculous Riddles*. Des Moines, Iowa: National Geographic Children's Books, 2012.

Internet Addresses

Giggle Poetry
http://www.gigglepoetry.com/

Enchanted Learning: Cat and Lion Jokes and Riddles
http://www.enchantedlearning.com/jokes/animals/
cat.shtml

Aha! Jokes: Animal Jokes
http://www.ahajokes.com/animal_jokes_for_kids.html

Index

A
Ancient Egyptians, 41, 43

B
birds, 4, 5, 11, 25, 27
black cats, 40, 41, 42
bobcats, 35
body language, 12, 17

C
canaries, 4, 11, 27
cheetahs, 30–31
Christmas Eve, 10
Cinderella, 10
cities, 10, 11
claws, 10, 29
Cleopatra, 41, 43
climbing, 15
colors, 6, 11, 28
copycats, 4
cougars, 33
counting, 16, 19

D
dogs, 11, 19

E
England, 41
Europe, 41
eyes, 6, 9

F
fleas, 5

H
hissing, 17

I
Internet, 16

J
jaguars, 28, 34, 35
Japan, 41

K
kittens, 8–11, 15

L
leopards, 28–31
lions, 20–23, 27
lynx, 33

M
mammals, 33
mammoths, 36
manes, 21, 23, 27
marmots, 33
meowing, 4, 5, 7, 15
mice, 5, 7, 9, 12, 13, 19, 39, 40
mountain lions, 28, 32, 33, 34, 35

O
ocelots, 34

P
panthers, 28, 32, 33, 35
parrots, 5
Persians, 7
playing, 14
prides, 22
purring, 7, 16, 40

R
rats, 13
roaring, 22, 24, 38, 40
rodents, 5, 7, 9, 12, 13, 19, 33, 39, 40
rosettes, 28

S
saber-toothed tigers, 36–39
Scotland, 41
scratching, 13
senses, 6, 9
sleep, 7, 11, 38
spelling, 16, 17, 18
swimming, 8, 24

T
tails, 17
teeth, 37, 39
tigers, 24–27
toucans, 25

U
United States, 41

V
vision, 6

W
whiskers, 12
wildcats, 30, 32–35
witches, 41, 42
worship, 41